PRAISE FOR
From The Heart O

I would like to acknowledge the profound impact of Shirley's poetry, which fearlessly confronts social issues while providing solace and understanding. Their unapologetic approach to addressing these pressing issues offers a voice to the voiceless and sparks crucial conversations for change. Additionally, I am deeply grateful for her heartfelt poem on grief, which resonated with me on a profound level, providing much comfort during a difficult time. Shirley has a remarkable ability to use her words to heal, empower, and inspire, and her contributions to the world of poetry are truly invaluable.

– Lupe Gonzalez Cruz

I've known Ms. Ilcken for 50+years. I have read several poems which she wrote in response to our conversations. Her poem, "A Good- Bye Journey," was written in response to my tour of duty in Viet Nam. She captured not only my feelings but those of my fellow service members. Another prime example is her poem, "The Man-Child," which is a prime example of the strain between a father and son. I always look forward to reading more of her poems because so many of them deal with life.

– James Feimster, MSgt, USAF Retired

I find Shirley Ilcken's poetry inspiring and humorous, but also gripping as she depicts the truth of human suffering.

– Aamina Maher, Former Secretary, Afiba Center

From The Heart Of A Girl
To The Soul Of A Woman

From The Heart Of A Girl To The Soul Of A Woman

Life's journeys through love, friendships, family, social injustice and miscellaneous thoughts

Poetry by
Shirley Anderson Ilcken

From The Heart Of A Girl To The Soul Of A Woman
© 2024 Shirley Anderson Ilcken
ISBN: 979-8-218-49940-2

First Edition, 2024

All rights reserved. No part of this publication may be reproduced, distributed, or transmitted in any form or by any means, including photocopying, recording, or other electronic or mechanical methods, without the prior written permission of the publisher, except in the case of brief quotations embodied in critical reviews and certain other noncommercial uses permitted by copyright law.

Printed in the United States of America

Edited by Faith Forrest
Cover & Layout Design by Camille Ora-Nicole

Self-published with the support of CLI Books

This book is dedicated to the many strong women in my life who held me up, kept me going, taught me well and are still circling around me in body and in spirit.

TABLE OF CONTENTS

    Acknowledgements   Xiii

LOVE

    The Introduction   4
    Our First Dance   5
    The Man In The Moon   6
    Season Of My Memory   7
    Continuous Spring   8
    Fear   9
    When You Go   10
    Secret Thoughts   11
    After Thoughts   12
    Feels Like # 9   13
    A Man   14
    Missing You   15
    Selfish Love   16
    My Everything   17
    Morning Flight   18
    Mind Play Of A Past Love   19
    Food For Thought   20
    Thinking Of You   21
    Get The Message   22
    Readying The Rain   23
    Robbed By Love   24
    My Man   25
    Talking To You   26
    This Joy   27
    Thank You   28
    A State Of Being   29
    Silence Is Not Golden   30

Retreat   31
Somethings Not Right   32
The Wedding   33
Been Had   34
Warm Sun   35
If   36
Good-Bye   37
Always   38
Feelings   39
Sensual   40
In A Little While   41
Liar Liar   42
Just As   43
How   44
Thursdays   45
Your Love   46
Once Upon A Time   47
A Travel Through Time   48
I Think I've Been Battered   49

FRIENDS AND FAMILY

Every Family   53
All My Children   55
Sister Mother Friend   56
High Hopes   57
My Little Lady   58
Tomodachi (Friend/Japanese)   59
Lunch Time Chill'n   60
The Man Child   61
Mama (#1)   62
The Great Divide   63
They Lived A Full Life   64

Where Did They Go   65
Thank You Fredrick Smith   66
My Baby   67
A Mother's Love   68
Nannies' House   69
Ode To Ophie   70
Daddy   71
Sameya   72
The Get Together   73
Beautiful   74
The Merry-Go Round   75
Mama (# 2)   76

SOCIAL JUSTICE

The Face   79
Rising   80
Undocumented Refugee   81
The Good-Bye Journey   82
Under Siege   83
The Race   85
Memorial Day   86
Good Morning   87
Gentrification   88
Lady Liberty Speaks   89
Audio… Visual   90
Africa   91
Shake It Up   92

INSIGHTS THOUGHTS DAYDREAMS AND IMAGINATION

I Heard My Sistahs Speak   95
Can You See   96
Resurrection   97

Representations 98
Moon To Earth 99
The Writing On The Wall 100
Ode To Ms. Mary Bailey Lanier 101
A History Lost 102
A Constant Battle 104
Imagine A Smile 105
Cloud My Mind 106
Hiding My Tears 107
Hu-Man 108
We Are 109
Claiming My Life 110
Out Of My Name 111

ACKNOWLEDGEMENTS

I must first thank God because I was not suppose to make it through the first few months of my life, my mother Olivia Butler Brasley who didn't give up on me and Zora Gray (the woman I called grandma) who helped care for me to the amazement of my doctors and nurses while my mom went to work and her daughter Phyllis Gray Fawcett who always saw me as her little sister.

To so many people, friends and family who got me to this place in my life, you all know who you are and those of you who have passed on but are still with me in spirit.

I can't forget the Sims Poetry Library and its CLI Program, its staff and students in my class and The CLI students I met at get-to-gethers.
You gave me the opportunity to experience an expanded world of poetry with people that looked like me.

From The Heart Of A Girl
To The Soul Of A Woman

Love

There are many types of love. Love can be of a person, place or thing. There is love as a young child, teenage type love and the committed type of love between two people that can lead to marriage or a lifetime commitment. Love can bring such joy and happiness but sometimes it can bring hurt, pain, sadness and heartbreak especially when a committed relationship dissolves. I am in no way an expert or authority on love, but I have had my share of both the joys and heartbreak side of love, along with being privy to the views shared by others or observed from afar.

THE INTRODUCTION

Let me introduce myself to you
My name is Love
I am funny I am witty
I am sensuous I am sexy
I can show you delight
In the simplest of pleasures
Make you sing, sway and dance
Without a note to ear
I can make cold rainy days
Feel like warm sunshine
Make your heart flutter and skip a beat
Put a swivel in your hips a dip in your stride
Scramble your mind
And make you feel like you're on cloud nine
And when I say good-bye
There may be tears sadness and pain
But you'll always remember me
And the first acquaintance we made

OUR FIRST DANCE

You take my hand and ask me to dance
I take your hand and take a chance
Your hand on my back, you pull me close
I reach to your shoulders and hold on tightly
The music plays and we begin swaying to its beat
I'm hoping we don't step on each others feet
They aren't playing our song but we dance on
Feels like I'm floating on air without even a care
I can hear your heartbeat, can you hear mine
You look down at me, I look up at you
Our eyes meet and with a soft kiss each other we greet
The music stops and there's something we both know
This dance will never end as long as we are spirits kindled

THE MAN IN THE MOON

The man in the moon I cannot reach
for he is just a myth in which many believe
The man of my dreams I haven't met yet
for he is only in the imagery of my dreams

The man in the moon I seek and want to meet
may not possess the qualities my dreams have
or will profess, may not be part of my immediate
or future reality

So I'll just keep dreaming, I'll just keep waiting
Until the man in my dreams becomes my reality

SEASON OF MY MEMORY

Taller than average
Almond colored
Baritone with a slight lisp
Bedroom eyes
A cool strut like Denzel
A gentle touch that causes quiver
For everything there is a reason
This is the reason for my season

CONTINUOUS SPRING

Continuous spring in my mind's eye
where hummingbirds fly to and fro
where flowers are in bloom and butterflies flutter

Continuous spring in my heart
received like incoming blood to its atria
then pumped through its ventricles keeping the flow

Continuous spring all around me
buzzing like the sounds of bumble bees
on their journey gathering nectar from the
blossoms of spring

FEAR

To be afraid to dance on a cloud
for fear danger beneath me abounds

To be afraid to walk in the rain
for fear droplets might turn into rain

To be afraid to bath naked in sun's rays
for fear some may think me crazed

To be afraid my heart might break
fearing forever a painful ache

Afraid to experience love again
for fear of encountering another end

WHEN YOU GO

When the time comes for you to go
am I supposed to forget about you or keep you in my heart,
forget our long walks, our countless
hours of conversation on varied topics,
the holding each other in warm embraces
and the tender passionate love making

When the time comes for you to go
do I cry… while asking why this you choose
was it something I said, something I did
or didn't do, something I should or
should not have done.

When the time comes for you to go
will you remember me as I remember you
will you remember us and all the time we spent
will you keep me in your heart or only think of me
as someone you once knew a long time ago

SECRET THOUGHTS

Thoughts of sensuality
making me softly smile
hoping no one can see
else they know I'm thinking
of thee

Thoughts of a gentle touch
sending me soaring high in flight
never wanting to come down
leaving ripples of warmness
and delight

Thoughts of embracing
all through the night
neither of us wanting to let go
until the early light of dawn

Thoughts of remembrance
of the flight and the longing
to relive again my secret delight

AFTER THOUGHTS

Thought the longing would leave
but it seems for you my heart still grieves

Thought the sighing would cease
but there's no relief for this exhale of yearning

Thought the wanting you near would disappear but this desire
is still quite clear

Thought the thoughts of you would dwindle
but my mind keeps running like a fast moving spindle

Thought the warm southern breeze would turn cool
but the thermostat still reads ninety-nine degrees

I thought the after thoughts would all be different
but they've become even more significant

FEELS LIKE # 9

Been given the potion # 9
I'm drunk in the glow
of love and bliss

Like the cat with nine lives
I've got a second chance
to live a new life

On a beauty scale of 1 to 10
I'm feeling like I was chosen
number nine

Dressed to the nines in joy
It's the highest degree this feeling you give me

A MAN

Gets into your mind and into your very soul
till your love fits him like a smooth leather glove
says deep down inside he's a very sensitive guy
misunderstood and doesn't know why
wants to live in your love
and return it by doing whatever to earn it
says you're the only one he really ever loved
and no other woman does he place above you
sends you through so many chasms
it makes your heart flip-flop with spasms
then says he needs some space
when he feels he is falling from your grace
cowardly at times
can't say what's really on his mind
more like jellyfish without a spine
finds it hard to confess
so not to be responsible for cleaning up his mess

MISSING YOU

Missing you is like…
A sky without the sun
A riverbed without water
Peanut butter without jelly
A mountain without a view
An ocean without fish
A heart without a beat
An ache without a cure
So incredibly awful to endure

SELFISH LOVE

There is no even yoke to bind
the pieces of this cloak
only a selfish love
not symbolized by the dove

No stairway to climb together,
only you as the ladder
to the status and success
that is sought

You are the way and means
to wants and needs,
solution to all problems,
not the companion
in common quests and dreams

The constant absence of your presence
is permitted in order to provide
the constant flow
of materials and treats

Yourself you've committed
to the acceptance of lifelong blame
while the other constantly exhibits
no guilt or shame

There is no even yoke
to bind the pieces of this cloak
only a selfish love
not symbolized
by the dove

MY EVERYTHING

You're my morning light
my pale moonlight

You're my winter storm
my springtime calm

You're my joyous laughter
my heartfelt tears

You're all my hopes
my dreaded fear of losing you

You're my very beginning
my forever to the end

You are… the rest of my life
my everything whole

MORNING FLIGHT

You took me on a flight just we two
Across the plains and oceans blue
Over tree tops and mountain tops
Higher and higher we flew
Feelings experienced all brand new
Too soon our flight would end
But relived in our minds over and
over again

MIND PLAY OF A PAST LOVE

Like the words to hip-hopp
The melody of bebopp
The game of hopscotch…
You invade my mind
You incite recall…
Forcing me to relieve it all

Like a childs nursery rhyme
Like the thinness of a dime
With the smoothness of oil…
You invade my mind
You incite recall…
Forcing me to relive it all

FOOD FOR THOUGHT

The table has been set
a scrumptious meal, a wish come true
presented just for you

You feast and you dine
on delicacies as fine as aged wine
till alas the cake you've eaten

With appetite now satiated
the feast has ended, body warmed,
the chill is no more
you've now become full
until you move on
to your next lovers feast

THINKING OF YOU

When I think of you I think of life
I think of love and what it feels like

When I think of you I think of gentleness
of a soul full of warmth and tenderness

When I think of you I think of the longing
I think of the wishing for belonging

When I think of you I think of what it would be
if you could feel like me

When I think of you I wish that for a little time
I could think of you as mine

GET THE MESSAGE

Get the message
he loves a challenge
it's his claim to fame
the greater the challenge
the greater his game

He is in it to win
it doesn't matter
who he has to pin
as long as he wins
in the end

Can't you see
with him it's an art
yet you continue to give
all of your heart

Got the message…
the game is over
understand the action
You… were the challenge
his temporary distraction

READYING THE RAIN

I've felt the dew and fine mistiness
I've felt light drizzles and sprinkles
Now I ready myself, for the showers are about to descend
I've experienced hurt and pain
discontent and frustration
I've experienced the lack of what should have been
Now I ready myself, for the showers are about to begin
This… is the beginning of our end

ROBBED BY LOVE

Robbed of my youth and my girlish figure
of my sweet gentle smile
walking now with my face in a scowl

Robbed of my innocence of life
to experience years of strife
Love robbed me of my sensitivity
and left me to exist in a cold constant blizzard
...was this my destiny?

Robbed of my offspring
they now live in the isms of today's society
commercialism, materialism, selfism

Robbed of my tears
the well drained bone dry early on
Love robbed me of my spirit and all that went with it
and sentenced it to limbo until freedom releases it

MY MAN

My man will know me as I am, with my milieu
of relaxed fit jeans, loose fitting tops,
comfortable shoes and for the sweet honey
and passion that lies within

He will be strong within and accept my strength
as I stand beside him, he'll know
I am there to be his shoulder to lean on
his support when his strength sometimes wanes or falters

My man will have a sense of humor but not too dry
and he'll make me laugh when my spirit gets low
because he knows I'll be his comfort and joy
when his spirit, mind or body feels low, rundown or blue

He will be my mate in mind, body and soul
because he will know I am his mate in the same
and that our love is true, our love is real
not a play of game, not a temporary thing

My man will treat me like his queen, his favorite fantasy
because he knows he'll always be my king, my sole desire,
the sweet honey and passion that lies within me

TALKING TO YOU

Talking to you is like walking on air
like floating on a cloud above the crowd
making me feel I am wearing a crown

Talking to you is like being in another world
like sun shining through on a rainy day
makes me imagine springtime in May

Talking to you is like eating chocolate
like sipping a hot toddy at bedtime
makes me want to savor the sounds
of smoothness and warmth

Talking to you is like a good nites sleep
like breakfast in bed, such a nice treat
makes me cast all my cares away
to ready for challenges of the day

THIS JOY

Making me jump
I can't sit still but I don't want
any tranquilizer pills

Taking my mind away
from tasks of the day
taking it back to the past

words keep coming
daylight thru the night
making me write as
fast as I can

Taking me through
a myriad of fantasies
this strange malady
don't want to come back
too soon to reality

THANK YOU

Thank you for putting my head back on straight
I should have paid attention from the gate

Thank you for fracturing my heart again
seems with you it's an art well penned

Thank you for the tears you made me cry
they are washing away the clouds covering my eyes

Thank you for the warm breezes you made me feel
they prepared me for the big chill

Thank you for the temporary moments of laughter
sharing and pretentious caring

My head is back on straight again
next time I'll pay more attention at the gate

A STATE OF BEING

In a state of bewilderment
baffled and befuddled
causing disorientation in
time and space

In a state of perplexity
thought puzzled with
complicated pieces and
where they fit

In a state of confusion
disconcerted and muddled
permitting mental and emotional
disturbances

Crazy, confused and psychotic
puzzled and enigmatic
this complexing feeling of
being in love

SILENCE IS NOT GOLDEN

The phone calls lessen, letters almost non-existent
the lines of communication are growing silent

The excuses grow in number and make me start to wonder
why the lines of communication have grown silent

You say one thing and then another and act like that old cat
the one who swallowed his tongue

Silence isn't always golden as the old folks use to say
one needs to be careful or love may decay

RETREAT

You have fought in battles with men and guns
You have fought in jungles of green and concrete
Battles with foes and yes some with friends
Some physical while others verbal
You fought the past with courage and determination
Now this sort of fight causes you great frustration
Do you retreat, do you withdraw, do you lose what
is special and good, will you stand firm and fight off defeat
or alas from love you will always retreat

SOMETHINGS NOT RIGHT

I fear something's not right
something in your quietness, in your voice
something's not typical in this conversation

I'm trying to see through the mask
I'm trying to figure out the days
of your most recent past

Are we right or are we wrong for each other
do you again feel hypocritical
and dread that you they will ridicule

Is it something I said or did
talk too much or of your time
demand of such

Do my outlets of emotion become
too much of an explosion, is my reality
to you more than a notion

I'm trying to see through the mask
trying to figure out the days of
your most recent past

Something's not right, I felt it all night
you are my destiny and for you
I wholeheartedly fight

THE WEDDING

Missed the high one gets
from reading, the colors,
the flowers, the words that empower

Missed the hugs, the kisses,
the congratulations and dedications,
the food, the drink, old folks' winks

Missed the clicks, the flashing
of the cameras, instructions to
move this way and that

Missed all the guest with gifts
they beard but most of all
I missed me there

BEEN HAD

You sat by the wayside and each day cried
He cusses, hits and kicks
While you hardly get a good night's rest
He gets all his best
You tried to be the loving, dutiful wife
Taking all the blame when there was strife
This is the thanks for giving your whole life
You toss and you turn
Wishing in hell he'll burn
What a lesson through the years
His love was never real
There's a time to let go
A time to realize
You've been had

WARM SUN

On this winter's day with crisp breeze in the air
I sit in the warmth of the sun while my mind turns to
thoughts of you

On this winter's day with a crisp breeze in the air
my heart rests in the warmth of your love
that feels like a well fitted glove

Warmth that fills my body from head to toe
warmth that makes my outsides glow
makes my spirit light and everything bright

IF

If I could be as free as a breeze
to blow wherever I so pleased
would you love me then

And if I could learn
half the things you've learned
could you love me then

If my conversations were not weak
and on varied topics I could speak
would you love me then

And if the color of my skin
were the color of your skin
could you love me then

GOOD-BYE

They tell me in your family's ties
you must all see eye to eye

That in this type of situation
we could be no more than friends

They tell me I should find another
and this time make it a "brother"

But maybe when we meet again
I can be more than just a friend

Adiós amigo, hasta luego
until we meet again

ALWAYS

There will always be an empty space
a void that you can't seem to fill
with highs nor thrills nor pills

There will always be a curve
in your lip, a rise in your eyebrow
as you ponder the time well spent
and the time not spent

There will always be that one wish
you'll wish could be granted
if only you could find a genie
to command it

As you close your eyes to sleep at night
I will be that soft little light, the one
you'll always see even with your eyes shut tight

You'll always see my symmetry in shadows
and my spirit will dance in the chambers
of your mind, never to be locked
in the shadows of time

Your heart will always be half not whole
Because I will always be
that part of your soul

FEELINGS

Although I am in love
I sometimes feel alone

I listen for the sound of the telephone ring
but there's no tone of a bell to be heard

I listen for the sound of the gate when pushed open
but peering out the window there's no one there

I listen for the sound of your knocking at my door
but it's only the delivery man leaving a package

Although I am in love
I sometimes feel alone

SENSUAL

Feelings deep inside dormant and silent
then love came knocking at my door
I obliged and reciprocated

Like a crater of hot molten lava
bubbling and steaming inside
slowly, silently, un-methodically creeping

My senses awakened, heightened to
the touch of his hand, whispers in my ear,
the sight and smell of our bodies entangled

My womanhood sings joyously
with an explosive release of feelings
and the thoughts of his passion within

IN A LITTLE WHILE

In a little while my eyes will dry
the pieces of my heart
will mend again

In a little while I can listen
to sad love songs on the radio
and not relive the pain

If I had a little more time
I might be able to forget
that I ever loved you

Just give me a million years
and then maybe it will seem
like just a little while

LIAR LIAR

Contemplation, mitigation
of thoughts, actions, truths and lies

Instigation, litigation
on behalf of deeds done wrong

Conniving in order of deriving
at conclusions for your delusions

You blame and hurt
and at most times you are very curt

Skirting issues when it comes to real feelings
thus resorting to double dealings

Life would be much more thrilling
if you'd be more willing

You need to mend your ways
before the passing of too many days

One never knows when the end is near
and misses experiencing us being near

JUST AS

Just as the flowers
with their varied fauna and colors
Love has many forms

Just as the flowers that bloom
in spring and throughout the year
Love should be ever growing
in heart and mind

Just as blossoms of flowers need
care for longevity love needs care
and nurturing for endurance and
growth to last a lifetime

HOW

How can one see love if he will not open his eyes
to the sights it brings
A sight of beauty in the everyday people
And all the things to see around your world
How can one hear the sounds of love
when he will not turn an ear to listen

There are sounds of joy and laughter
Sounds of sighs and cries
How can one feel love when he will not turn the key
in the lock that shields his heart

Feelings of happiness bubbling over
Feelings of sadness when it's over

THURSDAYS

A day of anticipation and longing
A day that never seems to end
The day before Friday

A night of sweet remembrance
The night of endless yearning
A night of sleeplessness
The night before Friday

The night before I hold you in the flesh
The night before our journey begins again
The night before Friday

YOUR LOVE

Joy has filled me up from head to toe
Peace has mellowed me from inside out
Your love has lifted my heavy heart

My walk is feathery, my speech is calmer
My laughter is heartier, my glass
is no longer half full… it's overflowing

My happiness is in abundance
Dreams are plentiful in occurrence
Your love… has made this possible

ONCE UPON A TIME

Once the pain was gone
now it has returned

My feelings of fullness
are now of emptiness

My feelings of happiness
have all turned to sadness

Once upon a time I had a
love now I have lost him

A TRAVEL THROUGH TIME

By accident or by design
You entered my life the very first time

We walked, we talked, we became friends fast
That's when my heart took its fatal crash

We sat, we hugged with an occasional kiss
You never knew I was engulfed in bliss

Then came the time to say good-bye
I surely thought my heart would die

As the years went by I kept you close, often gazing
at your image captured, in hope one day
you'd heal my fractured heart

By accident or by design
You entered my life for the second time

We talked and laughed of things present and past
You finally know what I was so afraid to show

Now my fractured heart is on the mend
Because I have you back again… my old friend

I THINK I'VE BEEN BATTERED

I have no open wounds no scars
nor band-aids nor bruises
but I think I've been battered

It was early in our life
that my heart often ached
from the lack of your affection
and I wondered if there would ever be
any real joy or is this my fate

Is my mind playing tricks on me
Is this continuous emotional turmoil
really injected or is it imagined

Many times I cried from the words
that hurt, that cut like a knife
so many times I kept quiet out of fear
that the words would begin again abruptly
many times I felt I must walk like a mouse
in my own house
I have no open wounds no scars
no band-aids nor bruises
but I think I've been battered

My eyes must have played tricks on me
because the white horse this knight rode
was really black and the armor he wore
was rusted inside

I have no open wounds no scars
nor band-aids or bruises
but I finally realize
I have been battered

Friends and Family

A family is something to be cherished even though at times they don't get along with each other. Being part of a family can bring you a sense of wellbeing, love grief or strife.

Family doesn't have to be blood relatives or family through marriage. It can be a unit of individuals who provide all the same as a traditional family, the sense of love, wellbeing, nurturing and the like.

Friendship like family is also something that should be cherished, but be aware that true friends and acquaintances are not the same. True friendship, real friendship is much stronger and binding for a lifetime, never forgotten, even with distance or death.

A true friend will always lend an ear, comfort you in sadness or distress, celebrate in your joys and check you when your wrong or out of control, just as a family would.

EVERY FAMILY

Every family is the same
the only difference is in the name
There's... you know his name
Whose claim to fame is his ability to imagine
far beyond the rest if you know what I mean
In short, he is The Family Liar

Then there is auntie what's her face
Whose been everywhere, done everything
and knows how to do everything
and anything no one else can do or had done before
Her name is Auntie Know It All

There are sisters and brothers of sorts
Who find it hard to get a job or keep a job
they mooch, borrow and live off other family members
We shall call them The Lazy Good For Nothings

Let us not forget that particular member
Who never learned to drink out of a cup... so to speak
and is good at hiding himself and his problems
in the bottom of glass bottles of particular brand names
He is known as The Family Drunk

Then there are those family members who possess
lots of money, material wealth and such
whether earned or inherited and tend to
always want to lord it over everyone else
They are known as The Family Snobs

And please let us not forget that one old uncle
Who can't seem to keep his mind, hands and eyes
off some other man's woman instead of on his own woman
His name is Uncle Playboy

Last but not least there are the old folks
one or two who always want to bend your ear

with the same old stories you've heard a million times
about some fable, proverb or something that happened long ago
They are known by many aliases such as The Family Griots
Wise Ones, Storytellers and Keepers of Family History

So you see, there is not need for embarrassment
nor discontent about your placement in this membership
Just remember every family is the same
The only difference is in the name

ALL MY CHILDREN

You came in for help and stayed a while
you of many ethnicities and different ages
All my children

One day you'll stray to find your own way
always returning at one time or another
All my children

Some of you will call to say hello, to say thanks
and to know there's still a safe place where you can go
All my children

The day will come when each other we'll seek no more
but keep the memories in our minds back door…
All of you, always my children

SISTER MOTHER FRIEND

You were there in my tiny beginnings
You shared with me your mother
My grandma she fast became
I part of your family
All of yours became mine

Sometimes you dragged me along
At times you wished I weren't there
My big sister you soon became
Always there for my joys and tears
Always there to lend an ear

Extension of your family, extension of mine
Forever our families to be intertwined
Always having to explain how it all began
This relationship between us will always be
My sister… my mother… my friend

HIGH HOPES

I had high hopes they'd not be like me
but be the best they could be

I had high hopes they'd not settle for less
but reach for the sky

High hopes they'd not just compete
but strive to attain many amazing accomplishments

I had high hopes for them but at times
they seemed to be afraid they'd be just like me

MY LITTLE LADY

My little lady average height but petite for her age
followed her dream to change it all because
she wanted to play flag football

To the other parents' chagrin and disdain of the coach
conviction and abilities won her a place on the team
but hardly allowed her off the bench for long

The final game of the school year was in play
the team losing badly during the final quarter
a win didn't look promising at all

To all our surprise it was the fathers who put their egos aside
and yelled "put Christina in the game"
and the coach obliged

Showing power and prowess she ran weaving in and out
she led her team to the win never thinking she was ever less
than the boys, never listening to all the noise of those not in
agreement of her quest

TOMODACHI (friend/Japanese)

Friend forever for eternity
Spirits made kin early in our friendship
by fate or by God's plan

Through highs and lows
through thick and thin
in joys and now in sorrow
beyond the end

You taught me patience
and the importance of humility
you showed me a world outside my own
bringing experiences I would not have known

Now, as before I try to think and hope
I had given a part if not as much to you in return
knowing there are few in this world who had or
will ever have the honor of knowing a friendship
like ours

Though this is good-bye to what was on this earth
I will look forward and continually to the spirit
And friendship we'll still share through eternity
Sayonara Tomoko-san

LUNCH TIME CHILL'N

Sit'n back, laid back
grease'n and kick'n it
with my girls

Chat'n bout what's just ill'n us
peep'n this and peep'n that
and g…i…r…l, what chu say

Well, ya know it's been real
no mo time ta chill back to da j-o-b
guess we bess be hit'n it

THE MAN CHILD

Wanting to be all on his own
thinking he is just too grown
a man-child in his own little world

Never venturing to seek guidance
from those who care but from those
who see life as one big dare

This man-child you so deeply love
now to be treated with kid gloves
so not to wound his false pride

For if you bark he will surely dart and run
not understanding you are giving him
grounds for safe landing

Hardly a call to speak of love or
to say I miss you dad but thoughts
or deeds that will frisk you

This man-child brought into the world
with a road map for much success
chooses to live on the edge of distress

To become a man is a journey in itself
one can only hope this child becomes a man
before he is forced to take that last stand

MAMA (#1)

Mama, I'm the child your raised
the good girl, the one you put your trust in

Mama, I'm the responsible child
the one you could always depend on

I'm that sweet, loving child
the one ready to give emotional support of any sort

Mama, I'm the adult you raised
if only you would cooperate

You make me feel like I am in a constant haze
like a zombie in a daze

I wanna be productive in seeking care for you
but all you do is force me to bear with you

Mama, I wanna give you the rest of your life in comfort
and care but you won't let me take you there

THE GREAT DIVIDE

By birth we were sisters born of same mother
under the same roof we spent most our lives
one room we shared each our own side
the rug and the dresser being our divide

Personalities so different and so often compared
you like our mother, always outgoing and fun loving
I the quiet one too shy and reserved to let go
in our youth, so near and yet so far apart

A pathway perpetuated a lifetime divide within our hearts
though I always loved you, seems you never really loved me
never able to look up to you and you looked down on me
once coming together with the birth of my first

All seemed forgiven, pushed and locked in the past
thought we'd be close sisters at last
then something happened, I don't know quite what
our ties that became close would now be cut

Divided again, guess we just can't pretend
those differences keep interfering with us being friends
so you'll go your way and I'll go mine
seems we'll never fill this perpetual divide
know I still love you and always will
maybe in our next lives this divide will be filled

THEY LIVED A FULL LIFE

They lived a long life
these makers of our history long ago
and not so long ago
We want to hold on and not let go
because they make our lives full
and our lifes' journeys more bearable
They lived a full live
with hopes and dreams, loves, losses
maybe some hardships, trials, tribulations
but they journeyed through it all
They lived a full live
Some journeyed from far away
others from not so far away
while some took their journeys
in the place of their birth
We want to hold on and not let go
because they make our lives full
and our lifes' journeys more bearable
They lived a full live
leaving us a recipe for living
a recipe for making love long lasting
a recipe for laughter and joy
recipes which we can take from and add to
We want to hold on and not let go
but their journeys' have come to an end
an all new journey awaits them in a spirit that will never die
We want to hold on but with sorrow or heavy hearts we must
let go…
our journeys are not yet over
we must continue on

WHERE DID THEY GO

Where did my children go
they were once here with me
they were once happy and smiling
they were loving and caring
eager and willing to learn
they have all but disappeared
could it really be me… as they say
what could it be?

Where did my children go
once they were here with me
now they are bitter and angry
now they are single minded
insensitive and mocking
they have all but disappeared
could it really be me… as they say
what could I've done better
what could I have done more of?

THANK YOU FREDRICK SMITH

My thanks to you Fredrick Smith
for calling me out on many occasion
to shine the light I would not shine

You introduced me to a community
of like whose lives were made of words
built on thoughts and imaginations

Your belief helped to ease my fears
thus allowing me to write my words as they come
to sound my words so others can hear

Though I might not go as far as you hope
I will never forget you and your encouragement
as I cheer you on in your pursuits, dreams
and quest

MY BABY

She's my baby
So little, so helpless
With eyes so big and bright

She's my baby
Growing so strong
All smiles and coos
My precious little jewel

She's my baby
Running or walking
Laughing or crying
And soon she'll be talking

She brought joy to my life
And until she becomes a wife
She'll still be "my baby"

A MOTHER'S LOVE

A mother's love is always there
Even when you think she doesn't care
A mother's love is tried and true
Even when we make her feel blue
She swallows her pride and hides her pain
Even when we cause her pain
She'll give up her last and do without
Give up her rest so we can have the best
A mother's love will never die
No matter how much of her nerves we try

NANNIE'S HOUSE

Babies crying wanting to be held or fed
children's laughter as they played inside
and outside the house
young and old dancing in the living room
to music spinning on the record player

Pots continuously being scraped and refilled
as family take turns sitting to eat
at the dining room table …File Gumbo
being the dish most sought

Dominos table slapping, card players yelling
sports fanatics congregating in the small den
to watch televised games back to back throughout
the day while others move throughout the rooms
making conversation where they can

Crying, playing,
eating, laughing, talking …
Nannie's house on Thanksgiving Day

ODE TO OPHIE

Always ready to lend an ear
To our questions or concerns
Giving advice whether naughty or nice
on topics and discussions of the day

Sometimes you want to be left alone to mope or brood
and there's nothing we can do to change your mood
But most times you're ready to have fun
at the drop of a dime

Helpful in so many ways, bringing solace to a place
where we must spend most of our waking hours
You keep us going throughout the work day
making us laugh and giggle as if still young girls
sometimes getting reprimanded for being too loud

DADDY

You always came to visit me, mama didn't know
Grandma keep our secret so you I could see
Sit there till you sober up she'd say to you
then your daughter you can greet
we'd sit talking you and me
though of what I can't remember much
Gramma said I looked like your sister, I only saw her once
Too soon you passed away and I watched the procession
of cars from the school yard fence
You must have felt the pain I felt
for you obviously begged Gods pardon and
from purgatory you were released to visit me again
You knew I was really sad and needed a friend,
needed my dad
You set the record straight when no one else
even thought to dare
They don't know how I came to know about what came before
what was kept behind closed doors
I think of you often and wishing in my adult life
you could have shared
then maybe from so much of my childhood
I would have been spared

SAMEYA

Sameya, grandma waits to see your little face
if you're short, if you are long
if you'll be fat or small

Sameya, grandma waits to see your smile
to hear your cry as you enter this world

Sameya, grandma is waiting to look into your eyes
to hold your little hands, to caress your cheeks

Sameya, grandma is waiting to hold you near
to rock you in her arms, to sooth your little soul
when at first this new world becomes a little too much

Sameya, please come soon, please come now
grandma is waiting

THE GET TOGETHER

Family, old friends and a ride along guest
to be deemed family through association

BB King and Bobby Blue Bland playing in the background
with feet tapping and testification to their words
This…. a signal to "let's get this party started"

Communication of all sorts going on
with laughter, exclamations and jive talking to one another

Whist players at the table intent with concentration
domino players follow suit outside
while sounds played by the younger generation
fill the air

Kitchen busy serving up good 'ol down home cook'n
every now and then a yell can be heard
"everybody doing ok?"
With stomachs now content, R&B along with a little funk
now playing
folks get relaxed and laid back

Conversation continues on the topics of the day
with music and laughter chiming in

…This is enjoyment at its best

BEAUTIFUL

You are sister, mother and friend
faithful and trustworthy
as your arabic name denotes

Your wisdom and knowledge
are bountiful, hence deriving from
experiences and pages of your life

Steadfast and a force
to be reckoned with, yet
possessing a heart of gold

Caring and empathetic
a spirit that shines brightly…
all who know you will testify

You are strength
you are grace and passion
with all said and done….
You're a beautiful woman
Named Aamina

THE MERRY-GO ROUND

Painted ponies of different colors
round and round they'd go
with music playing as they circled

Laughter and smiles I feel on my face
as he waves to me... this our
Sunday after church outing

This memory will never die
as I try to prepare myself daily
for his final breath but not a good-bye

His body no longer to be
but his spirit and this memory
will always be with me

MAMA (# 2)

If I could give you a field filled
with all your favorite flowers
...I would

If I could give you back the strength
and the spirit you use to have
...I would

If I could take away the hurt and all the pain
that life be felt on you
...I would

If I could mend your broken heart
and all the bad feelings
...I would

Mama, the one thing I can do
is to love you forever
...and I do

Social Justice

The world has been in a sort of turmoil, so to speak, for a good while. Many people have experienced injustice at one time or another in their lives, be it by an individual, a group, or the political system. Injustice because of race, ethnicity, economic status, gender, sexuality, or age.

THE FACE

I saw your face, the face of pain
So many wounded, so many dead

I saw your face, the face of anguish
So many boys won't become men

I saw your face, eyes filled with tears
The ones mothers cry when their children die

I saw your face, the face of anger, questioning
why are we here amidst all this danger

I saw your face, the comfort and caring
Especially for those you'll soon be burying

RISING

Women, we are rising
Around the world we are rising
We have heard the call of spirit

We have felt the desires of our sisters
We have felt the urgency of our true destinies
not those chosen for us, placed upon us
by masculine or societal oppression
of our thoughts, of our spirit
of who we really are and what we can become

Women around the world know
that we are powerful and we will not
be held down anymore by masculine ideals,
by society's ideals of who we are relegated to be

Women… we are rising
Around the world we are rising
And will continue to rise despite
threats, ultimatums or coercions
We are rising… rising… rising

UNDOCUMENTED REFUGEE

THEY will save your life
when you've fled your countries
hunger and strife

THEY will make sure
there is an outpouring of sympathy
in the name of humanity

THEY will roll out the red carpet
when from your countries you've been
expelled, exiled for political beliefs

AND when you arrive
make it fast and easy for
you to survive and strive

THEY will open their arms
and welcome the newly
arriving refugees...

EXCEPT if they look like you or me

THE GOOD-BYE JOURNEY

I came on this journey to visit the Memorial Wall
To walk my past in order to live in the present

To say good-bye to innocence lost
and the carefree days of my youth

Good-bye to the lies they told us and
to the senseless killings that for some became thrilling

Good-bye to the ideals of peace they preached
and the enemy we fought so desperately to defeat

Good-bye to comrades and friends with whom I stood
You died so young and would never know
what you could have become

Good-bye to all the sadness and pain
To the remembrance of sights still lodged in my brain

Good-bye to all pieces and parts of this game
I refuse to carry with me any portion of its shame

For I was a boy, as many were
Unknowingly used as a pawn
In this game called... VIETNAM

UNDER SIEGE

Under siege is what we are...
with constant wars and continuous battles
fought across lands in faraway places
taking our minds away from the realities
of our living day to day existence

Our youth being constantly reminded they are not whole
unless they possess the latest this or that
regardless of the cost to life, limb or financial stability
They are under siege

The poor and homeless sick, live in squalor on the streets
or pay exorbitant rents to greedy land lords
while living in insect rodent infested rundown buildings
We try to stay healthy at best but
foods are being laced with harsher pesticides
genetic modification and the manufacturing
of fake foods are proliferating
We are under siege

Education of our children has fallen by the
the wayside or almost left to chance and then
they're labeled slow or educationally retarded
least they don't stand a chance to move forward
to advance to a brighter future
Our children are under siege

Middle class folks finding it harder to make ends meet
when employers close up shop and move overseas
many laying off large numbers of employees
to enhance, intensify and swell their profits
resulting in our loss of home, health or life
We are under siege

Politics as usual is most times the scenario
using our numbers to put themselves in office
while pushing and promoting an agenda

of great expectations and promises as
"The great white hope" needed to improve or
eradicate our current circumstances
disproportionate to the status quo

PEOPLE... open your eyes, look around
open your ears, listen to the rhetoric
to the half-truths and outright lies
PEOPLE... We Are Under Siege

THE RACE

I've been running this race as long as I can remember
been passed up, passed by, passed over
though there have been times when the finish line
I almost crossed over

The miles have been long and many a bumpy road
my legs are not as strong as when I was younger
running all this time and now I'm without even a dime
what a waste of my precious time

Just as I approach the finish line there always seems
to be someone waiting who throws me a snag
instead of the flag, so I'm back at the beginning
and again at the lag

MEMORIAL DAY

A day of celebration
of picnicking, BBQ'ing
the sand and the waves

A day to mourn and remember
husbands, fathers, sons and daughters
who fought and died for country

A day of anger at the greed of men
and the arrogance that spent their
egos to calculate and deliver
such an atrocity as war

A day of regret and reflection
could the masses have stood up
and said, "no"?
will they stand next time and say,
"Absolutely no, we won't go"

GOOD MORNING

Good morning, Mrs. Smith
I see you're here regarding
the job listed on our bulletin board

You seem to be very qualified
and I can assure you this job
will never be a bore

There is one thing more, Mrs. Smith
punctuality is a must and new employees
with children we just can't trust

Good morning, Mrs. Smith
this apartment is very nice, look it over once or twice
you can see how much work it took indeed

Oh! There is one thing more, Mrs. Smith
in our building tenants with children
do not exist and on this rule I must insist

Good morning Dr. Jones, my name is Mrs. Smith
I am in a bit of a fix and I think you can be of help to me
you see Dr. Jones, I'm in need of a hysterectomy

GENTRIFICATION

I am raising my fist against gentrification
to the ones coming into my neighborhood
with sights of taking over, erasing havens
that provide glimpses of our past accomplishments
and our current cultural history in community

I raise my fist to you, the gentrifiers
whose great grandparents, grandparents
and parents fled the neighborhoods
when my people arrived seeking a place
to raise and grow their families

Not wanting to live amongst us
not wanting to get to know us
you now come back as to reclaim what was left
for us… the Black and Brown

I raise my fist to you, the gentrifiers
who have returned and built high wooden fences
and tall green hedges in order to block
your view of us and our neighborhood

Go back from whence you came
to the places your families fled to
but if you want to stay here and live amongst us
you should be willing to learn about our cultures
and who we really are

Gentrifiers, I don't want to raise my fist
and shake it at you, but want to welcome you
in community because I'm not going anywhere
I'm staying put

LADY LIBERTY SPEAKS

LONG AGO, I was placed on your harbor island
as a symbol of the democracy represented
I welcomed those who ventured to this place, the US of A
announcing liberty, freedom and democracy for all
just as its stars and stripes represented

WITH my arms open wide I held my lighted torch
as a guide to my golden door and announced for all
to bring me your tired, poor and huddled masses
those who crave to be free from oppression,
impoverishment

I SIGNALED the opportunity to start a new life that brings
stability and economic gain as you climb to success
ALAS, time has passed, my arms are still open wide
my light still guards the pathway thru the golden door
BUT I no longer want your tired, your poor nor your
huddled masses

I don't want those who suffer from adversities
ONLY send me your rich and well to do
the ones that have money and status
the ones whose descendants had eyes of blue
YOU SEE, I don't have blinders over my eyes, but
You have to realize I must now follow the status quo
SO if you don't fit the profile, then back to your countries
YOU must go

AUDIO... VISUAL

There was a time when what we saw and heard
was projected intentionally and deliberately
because of the color of our skins or ethnic identity

A perpetual atmosphere of non-inclusion
of people that look like me on the TV and in the movies
And when included skilfully designed and aimed at
presenting characters so unperceptive but
convincingly believable with suggestive implications
that we are nothing more than drug dealers, pimps,
prostitutes, shiftless and lazy good for nothings,
alcoholics who abuse their women and women who
don't know how to take care of their children

Audio...Visual many times seeming so malicious
as to causing us harm, injuries or death by the hands
of those who only believe stereotypes of who we are
At times the political system was organized tackfully
to keep most of us down, in our place, as it was called
assisting in preventing economic growth and mobility

The audio and visual inputs to our psyche and those of others
were discriminating, biased, prejudiced... racist

AFRICA

Africa take me as I am instead of looking down on me
you are the land, the country of my ancestors

Africa, I am you and you are me
we are your brothers and sisters
whatever has come to be and whatever will come to be

Africa, you say we do not know our history
our languages, our customs, our religions
but realize Africa, you do not know the real history
the history of how we got to the places we arrived at

Africa, we were taken against our will with force
by peoples of other lands and sometimes by our own
our languages of many became fewer and fewer, our customs
and religions not allowed to be practiced
except in secret

Africa, do not dismiss the fact that most of you had, and have
been shackled in mind and manipulated with many false
histories and histories purposefully left out of your story

Africa, we were once strong, proud and valued amongst
our communities as you all were before the continuous
attempts at at systematic genocide of minds, bodies and spirit

Africa, love and embrace us
as we have done you in our quest to know
and learn who we were and who we really are

Africa, we are you and you are us
we are your brothers and sisters
you are our brothers and sisters
take us as we are instead of looking down on us

SHAKE IT UP

Shake it up Black and Brown
all peoples of color
shake up the system not each other
shake up the system and stop allowing it
to shake you up

Shake it up in your hoods and neighborhoods
shake it up by coming together
stop the fighting and the killings over
so-called territory you legally don't own
begin and end with reconciliation and resolution

Peoples of color, together we are a force to be reckoned
why do you think we are constantly bombarded
with lies, misrepresentations and prejudices
about each other from each other, perpetuated
constantly in the public's mind by various media avenues

In prisons and jails they pit us against each other
it's all a rouse to divide and conquer, to keep us fighting
each other, to keep themselves in control while
some of our own follow their lead and their plan
they don't even understand they are also under control
in fulfilling their duties of dastardly inhuman deeds

Shake it up my Black and Brown, peoples of color
shake up the system not each other
watch, look, listen, take note from the past
while living in the present

Insights Thoughts Daydreams And Imagination

Sometimes we think about life, events and all sorts of things. Our thoughts can be triggered by words we hear, or something we see or read.

When we have an insight it can been seen as a deep thought, a strong feeling that can sometimes tell us something we need to know about ourselves or someone else or something else. It's the light bulb that lights up in our heads when we figure something out.

We all dream at some time or another, but usually at night when we sleep. Sometimes we dream during the day, when we stop and think of something in the moment that causes us to take our minds off of what we are doing… to the point that we may start staring out with a blank look on our faces, far away from what we were doing. Sometimes we might just sit quietly and transport ourselves into deep thoughts and imaginations of all sorts.

We've all had insights, daydreams and vivid imaginations at some time or another, not being conscious of it until later.

I HEARD MY SISTAHS SPEAK

I heard my sistahs speak last night
they warmed my soul
healed my heart
and made my spirit laugh

I heard my sistahs speak last night
they spoke of life
of living, of love
of joy, pain and agony
of wishes and remembrances
and regrets

these sistahs
chocolate brown
tan and caramel
tall lean and in-between
big boned, hefty and looking like me

I heard my sistahs speak last night
with varied doos
that speak of strengths they possess
the legacy they embrace

I heard my sistahs speak last night
they showed me how to express myself
with variety and still be me
that it's ok to speak of losses
of pain, agony or shame
Of raw sexuality
of my own sensuality
and still be me

These sistahs spoke to me last night
and I thank them for desserts of such sweet delights

CAN YOU SEE

I can tell you stories of a past of long ago
and of present day
of sounds and sights that have been with me from my
beginnings
through my present plight

Much of my shell is worn and missing, but my frame is strong
I stand serene and majestic in my old age
amongst my tall friends who have shaded me
from the hot summer heat
cooling me with their swaying leafy branches
when evening breeze greets
and yes, some of them are older than me

There are children running and playing, jumping and climbing
on sacks stacked high
the laughter still rings in my hollow being
determined bodies outside in the fields
going through their daily motions
trying to make a living, trying to feed the family
and trying to survive

and sometimes on occasion, love would seek shelter
and sneak moments of solitude and bliss
within my walls

All the stories I could tell are still here inside my shell
life through the years might have been hell
but like the descendants of the families gone by
I too have survived

Though I am now battered and worn, my frame is strong
and I stand majestic among my tall friends
some of them older than me

RESURRECTION

Resurrect yourself
you are not who they say you are
you are not what they say you have done
only you can resurrect yourself

Come out of the darkness that you allow to blind your eyes
your mind, your spirit, your soul
their shame is not your shame, their guilt is not your guilt
their self pity is not your self pity,
their affliction is not your affliction
their torch is not your torch to carry or bear

Resurrect yourself and come out of the darkness
for there is always light at the other end of the tunnel
there is always a new day that dawns
with a new beginning and an end of the old

Resurrect yourself
you are not what they say you are
not what they say you have done
leave the darkness, the pain, doubt and any shame behind you
only you can resurrect yourself and come into the light
don't let their hatred heart become your heart
don't let their vindictiveness become yours
don't let their misguided thoughts and deeds
become your misguided thoughts and deeds

Only you can resurrect yourself
come out of the darkness, come into the light
don't let this darkness become your comfort spot
or the spot you run to hide in

Life is worth living in the here and in the now
you are alive, so live your life full
without your doubts, fears and misguided conceptions
resurrect yourself come out of the darkness and into the light

REPRESENTATIONS

We are beauty in our own right
We are in the shape of the
Udu, Djembe, Kpanlogo and
Talking Drum

Messengers of word
across lands, seas and oceans
through time and generations
messengers of peace and hope
joy, love, celebration
sadness and death

Mother earth to the world
nurturer of the spirit
counsel to old and young
men and boys, women and girls
sons and daughters
sisters and friends

We are soothing and melodious
yet we can be powerful
you can hear our roar
when it is time to stand ground
we call attention

Symbols of strength and survival
withstanding what most
could not have withstood

We are beauty in our own right
In the shape of the
Udu, Djembe, Kpanlogo
and the Talking Drum

MOON TO EARTH

I am here to help you dream
To make your imagination form and soar
Here to help when you can't find comfort
in your quest to sleep

Tell me your thoughts on things of the day
Tell me your wishes, hopes, things you aspire
to do, become or to accomplish now or in
the near future

Just look out your window and fix your sights
on that pale light shining up in the nighttime sky
I may be full, I may be half, I might just be
a sliver of light in the sky

And if at times I'm covered by clouds or fog
I am still there, just look my way
as you usually do and find that space
where my shadow would be

I'll always be here to help you dream
To make your imagination form and soar
To help when you cannot find comfort
in your quest to find sleep

THE WRITING ON THE WALL

The writings on the wall, they're out to get you all
you write the words, you write the lyrics
they push you up the ladder of fame
and you know have an image to uphold
you can be brash, be naughty, be bold
if anything happens you're not to blame
it's all part of your newfound fame

The writings on the wall, they're out to get you all
you push the music, you push the lyrics
you've made lots of money, own multiple homes
and many expensive cars and garages to hold them
you can buy almost anything your heart desires

But don't forget there may come a day when they feel
for them you no longer sing and this marriage will be over
with no sign of a future fling when you've outgrown
your britches, forgotten whose boss
this, my friend, will be your great loss

The writings on the wall, they're out to get you all
stop jump'n at the bait, pump'n out the hate
pump'n up the hype, all that talk'n bout the sex

save your money, invest wisely and stay out of trouble
with the law and remember there's always
someone in the shadows waiting
to be the 'THE NEXT'

ODE TO MS. MARY BAILEY LANIER

Like the waves that come crashing onto a beach
sometimes calm and soothing
at other times with fury and strength
The gentleness of your presence and demeanor
gives forth an aura that can overtake
but at other times showing strength and determination
Stepping up, giving all you've got while maintaining convictions
like a fine wine smooth and mellow, bold or hearty
in your company, one can be relaxed and chilled
Experience your outspokenness
or chime in with your laughter
Wise from living life as it presented itself from your beginnings
Wise from emotions, and from lessons learned
Wise from the strength of the Black Woman that smolders
but never dies
YOU… are one of many phenomenal women

A HISTORY LOST

We've come so far as a people
You've been shown the struggle
Told of the hardships throughout
A rich and troubled history no doubt

Our recent past handed down
Spoken of by grandparents
Reiterated by mothers and fathers
Seconded by uncles and aunts

The struggle to vote, to read and write
The quest and sacrifice, the ultimate fight
We won the right we so deserved
In these days we must still persevere

Yet you throw it all away and you
Show your ignorance to anyone who
Will grant you an audience and blame
Your disposition on others near

Though our rights have been won
An invisible block has been laid
A force that you must watch and map
Else you will cease and self destruct

Yet you throw it all away and you
Show your ignorance to anyone who
Will grant you an audience and blame
Your disposition on others near

You ignore the head for caution
You ignore the call for your restraint
You ignore all of the teachings
You have been taught
You give up the struggle and the pain
You give up the quest and the hardship
You give up the teachings that made
Us so strong as a people

You throw it all away and show
Your ignorance to anyone who will
Grant you an audience and blame
Your disposition on others near

A CONSTANT BATTLE

There's a constant battle in my life
A battle within myself
A battle about myself
A battle to live my own life

Do I stand to who I am
Sometimes believing, feeling I'm not enough
Comparing myself to everyone else
Trying to fit into their mold

The constant battle with my spirit
A spirit that strives to survive
That struggles to stay alive
Warding off being broken

This constant battle in my life
When my empath sometimes causes me strife
And moves me to give too much of myself
To help someone else, not realizing
When it's proper to keep quiet

A constant battle with my heart
Do I continue to open it up to feelings of love
Even though there's a good chance it might get
Broken and proceed without constraint or retreat
With much caution and not take a risk

The battle of aging, realizing there's no longer
An abundance of time left to follow all the dreams
Left behind me, or do I proceed with their pursuits
As if there is no end

Of these constant battles within me
There may not be a conclusion or answers
To which or how these battles will end
The conclusive path to follow cannot be determined
But there are options and my life hasn't ended yet

IMAGINE A SMILE

Imagine as a child your most
dirtiest, raggediest pair of tennis shoes
wad of favorite chewed up gum
the coolest, most ickiest bug
your first game ever won

Imagine as a teen the funniest trick
you played on your friend, that first
girl that made your face beam, the
the thrill of your first kiss, that special
dance you didn't miss

Imagine the first time you ever heard
your daughter say that forever special
word "daddy" and later realize she'll always
be your little girl… come what may

Imagine the first time you knew you
were having a son, someone to do
all that guy stuff with, someone to
just hang out with

Imagine the day all your hard work
finally paid off, the day you received
your bachelors' degree and thought
to yourself, "wow, this is really for me

Now imagine an even bigger smile
one that reaches across your face at
at least a mile, freeze that frame
and keep it near to gaze upon
when you need cheer

CLOUD MY MIND

I look for tasks to be completed
to make myself busy as so not to
think of you

I direct my stare away from the
sky and down to the floor so not
to think of you

Over my fears I play my music louder
to drown out my thoughts so not
to think of you

I fight my sleep to stay awake longer
and deprive myself of dreams so not
to think of you

Time wasted on deeds to confuse
energy spent to cloud my mind but
thoughts keep coming back to you

HIDING MY TEARS

I hide my tears
When I should let them flow
Trying to keep my emotions in check
So no one can read all the cards in my deck

I hide my tears in the presence of alumming death
To show my strength, to show I am strong
And I can handle it all

In the face of adversity
While trying to show courage
I'm crying inside with anger and fear
To not to break down with a full angry cry

I hide my tears when I should let them flow
Because as a child was told crying makes
You have an an ugly face with eyes red
And with gray looking streaks left on
your brown skinned face

So I'll try to be strong even though
I may sometimes cry inside and I'll let my tears flow
On the outside

HU-MAN

Your wish is my command
but don't forget you are
only a man
human just like me

You have wants and desires
trials and tribulations, tests of the heart
and tests of courage

Your heart can ache, eyes can fill
with tears and you'll try to hold them back
out of fear your heart will experience
an emotional sear

Your wish is my command
but do not forget you are
only a mere man
human like I am

WE ARE

We are the children of Eve, not the blame
for Adams' misdeed, were created in the image
of the highest, with parts of Adam in our being

We populate the world, without us there would
be no human race, no mothers to comfort the
sick, those needing an ear, hug or warm embrace

We can bring home the bacon and still do
all things possible in a day if we choose
because the highest made us that way

We are the strength, as the real history can
read if it chooses to impart all our contributions
not just those of a few women inventors

We are the children of Eve, not the blame
for Adams' misdeed, created in the image of
the highest with parts of Adam in our being

So tell me why are we still usually the blame when
things don't go a man's way or the one responsible
to make his dreams come true

CLAIMING MY LIFE

Claiming my life as it was in my beginning
when surviving was the hardest, the strength
of a community that got me through it

I claim my life as I grew up with all my fears,
doubts and feelings of not being like mother
and sister, like cousins my age and near

I claim my life today all grown up with
less doubts and fears, less of trying
to be like my outgoing mother and sister

Today I claim the realization of close friends and
new communities that accepted me for me
and now I've finally claimed me as being me

OUT OF MY NAME

Descendants of the Spirit of the motherland
born in ceremony celebrated by community
given a name at birth with much meaning
many of joy, happiness, prosperity and
ancestral to be carried with us on our journey
through life... and Spirit rejoiced

One day, taken away by men who did not look like me,
who arrived in big boats from far away lands with guns
and whips chaining us to each other and forcing
us into their big boats... Spirit sobbed at the sight
of such brutality

Then my name was changed to one without meaning
changed to describe who owned us as their property
and I feared I would forget and not remember
who I am, who I was... and Spirit cried more tears

As much time passed on, my name was changed again
but this time by our own kind, selected by our mothers
from the names used by the descendants of
our captors... Spirit cried even louder

A great deal of time now passed, and our name
would once again be changed and again by our
own kind but not just by our mothers mouths
... Spirit wailed louder and profusely in anger and yelled

Saying... You were named at birth in the motherland
with names of profound meanings, these are your
mothers, grandmothers, aunties, sisters, nieces, and
all are spirit descendants of the Spirit of your
Motherland..." OUR NAME IS NOT BITCH"

Made in the USA
Middletown, DE
17 November 2024

64304590R00076